Every Day is An Act of Resistance

MONGREL EMPIRE PRESS
NORMAN, OKLAHOMA, UNITED STATES OF AMERICA

Norman, Oklahoma

2012

Cover Image: *Red Lady*
©2012 by Agneta Falk

MONGREL EMPIRE PRESS
NORMAN, OK

ONLINE CATALOGUE: WWW.MONGRELEMPIRE.ORG

This publisher is a proud member of

[clmp]

COUNCIL OF LITERARY MAGAZINES & PRESSES
w w w . c l m p . o r g

Book Design: Mongrel Empire Press using iWork Pages.

*For Alicia and Leah, and for Derek and "Katia,"
and for Clyde and Sadie*

ACKNOWLEDGEMENTS

Some of these poems have appeared in: *A Room of One's Own; Ball; Calling Home: Working Class Women's Writing, An Anthology; cold drill; Collision 3; Convolvulus No. 7; Compages No 21; Exquisite Corpse: A Journal of Books & Ideas; For A Living; Homeless Not Helpless; Journal of Women and Religion; Ikon; Lit. May 1994, A Literary Supplement of The San Francisco Bay Guardian; Modern Poetry Studies; News From Nowhere; People's Daily World; Portland Poetry Festival Anthology; Practicing Angles: A Contemporary Anthology of San Francisco Bay Area Poetry; Samisdat; The Spirit That Moves Us; Transfer/ 37; What We Hold in Common: An Introduction to Working-Class Studies; Womanblood: An Anthology of Women's Writing; Women's Voices; American Working-Class Literature.*

Every Day is An Act of Resistance

SELECTED POEMS

By

CAROL TARLEN

Edited by David Joseph and Julia Stein
With an Introduction by Jack Hirschman

CONTENTS

INTRODUCTION

In the twilight evening of June 29, 2004, that time of day and season in San Francisco when the air is both warm and chilly, some 80 people gathered in front of O'Reilly's Irish Pub on Green Street in North Beach to begin the celebration of the life of Carol Tarlen, who had passed away two weeks earlier. Though, in fact, Carol used to love to sit at the Pub's outdoor tables sipping a cocktail after her secretarial work, it was for another reason that the crowd gathered there that evening.

Across the street from the Pub is the Green Street Mortuary, where Carol had lain before being cremated, according to her wishes, a week before. The Green Street Mortuary is well known for providing a marching band for the families and friends of those who have died. Most of the funeral processions led by the band can be seen and heard going along Chinatown's Stockton Street on Saturdays and Sundays in the old New Orleans fashion. Traditional melodies are usually played—"Amazing Grace" or "Abide with Me"—and most of the processions are for Chinese Americans.

One of Carol's dying wishes was that the band lead a procession from Green Street three blocks down along Columbus Avenue to Specs Café, where she also liked to drink, and that "The Internationale," among other tunes, be played and sung as part of the ritual.

The band struck up the music—"When the Saints . . ." and other up-beat melodies—and when we arrived at Saroyan Alley, where Specs Café is, the band played "The Internationale" to many voices singing along with it, as well as labor and folk songs. Then we all entered the café where, for the next three hours, her comrades and friends publicly read Carol's poems or poems about her.

It was a beautiful farewell and tribute to a poet who had lived in North Beach for many years but who had resisted all the cliques and fashionables of that neighborhood—the street dope-poets, the Beats, and other etceteras. She was there, in fact living on the main drag, Grant Street, writing some of the best poems around, yet outside a few in the neighborhood who knew just how excellent her poems were, she was for the most part little regarded. Part of this was because this woman, an absolutely stunner in her youth, had been debilitated by a heart condition connected with serious diabetes that she had lived with since she was young and in her North Beach years she moved through the streets slowly and often hunched over. Her daughters and grandson lived in the neighborhood as well; she was happily close to them.

But the major part of the neglect of her as a poet was because Carol was not simply and steadily a worker at a 9-hour a day job, but she was a working class intellectual and proudly conscious of herself as such. Though the need to work for revolutionary change—a subject that, though given lots of lip service by many on the North Beach streets, usually ends up as blown bubbles of *Duh* or some-such shallowness, Carol dedicated her writing and her politics to help her class—the working class—her whole life.

Carol was a fighter. I'd met her in the Seventies at one of the poetry venues where she and her companion, the poet David Joseph, were reading. Then, in the Reagan years, we worked together on *Compages*, the magazine of translations of international poetry. Tarlen wasn't a translator but there were things that needed to be done at the sessions, especially the choosing of what translations would appear in the magazine. And later, she would work in the Communist Labor Party; Food Not Bombs where she got arrested for feeding the homeless; the League of Revolutionaries for a New America; the Labor Party's San Francisco chapter; her AFCSME union local at work; and as a union delegate on the S.F. labor council. She was a great voice for Union workers, got herself arrested at demonstrations, and wore a badge of pride on the Left side of her every moment.

Because her identity with the plight of workers was so strong—and she was not alone in this—she never grandstanded her work. Like many others, especially women, she put her class identity before her individual virtuosity, and so poetry and ambition never mixed in her. She was modest about her poems—though proud of them as well—preferring to talk about a collective action or the world situations or of what the women are doing. Because she was fiercely for women's rights—even if a fanatic San Francisco Giants supporter—she knew the double and treble burdens that capitalism dumps on women.

Her poems are the products of her feisty, ironic and always compassionate sensibility. While having little to do with the Beats, she is a product of that tendency, in Kerouac for example, toward direct confession, as in "Strangers", or toward an individuation of composition that at times reads like a *Grapes of Wrath* a generation later. That's perhaps because Carol's memories go back to days of being brought up in the trailer-park environments in Nevada (she'd joke about being "white-trash," and one of the poems of this book is so entitled), or because, at some time in her life, she realized that a poem is nothing if not the most honest expression of one's self.

It is her honesty indeed that is the winning aspect of the poetry. She engages in the direct confrontation with beings and situations with an often erotic determination, as at the end of the "Pt. Reyes Ode" that is dedicated to David Joseph:

> I'll reach for your sunburned skin
> my fingers climbing your thighs
> digging comfort from human
> soil, because I want to live
> with myself. You will rise
> to my hands. Celebrating one
> another, we will learn to forgive.

Those are very superb lines, without flourish or a sonority that might in fact get in the way of their fundamental intent: to reveal the immersion in another as the path to forgiveness itself. And note: the lines are very direct. The naming takes place without detours, as should be in such a situation. Tarlen remains faithful to the intimacy of the poem's necessity.

Whether she is writing about a direct confrontation with a would-be rapist, or a love poem, or the apocalyptic compassion of perhaps her most masterfully achieved poem, the "Sisters in the Flames" revelation of the true meaning of the Triangle Fire in the Lower East Side in the beginning of the 20th century, or the ever onward and upward lyric "Believe in My Hands (Which Are Ending)," she is able not only to evoke her own immersion in the materials, but, because of her deep honesty and sincerity in the process of the shaping of images as feeling, to draw the reader into the immersion as well. Her language, in its determined simplicity and directness, is the key that opens the depths of one's heart and soul to a radiant plunge into the human condition.

I am especially pleased in that respect to be able to introduce this important book of poems, the more so because it is the work of a woman and comrade who I hold in the highest regard as one with whose poetic and exemplary legacy, in word and deed, has contributed to preparing that revolutionary change so longed-for—and necessary —by and for all.

Jack Hirschman
Poet-in-Residence Friends of the San Francisco Library
Former Poet Laureate of the City of San Francisco 2006-2009

THE REBEL CALIFORNIA POET CAROL TARLEN
(1943-2004)

Carol Tarlen was a North Beach Emily Dickinson, publishing widely in magazines and anthologies but never putting out a full-length book. In the first section of well-known poem "White Trash: An Autobiography" her family is living in a trailer in Salinas when her younger brother gets dysentery and is taken to the local hospital: "After two weeks the doctors told my mother/to take him home to die./ Instead she took him to a university medical center. /He was given antibiotics and lived." Also, her father was a truck driver with narcolepsy, a disease that caused him to lose jobs, so the family was constantly moving around California until they settled in Fremont, in a blue-collar tract.

She knew her roots: knew her Quaker ancestors were indentured Anglo servants come from Britain to U.S. She took me to the Quaker meeting hall south of Market Street. She wrote a wonderful poem "In Circled Silence" paying homage to her Quaker ancestors "scorned, beaten, forcefed in prison darkness/Drenching a blinded nation with their/Inward Light." She knew about the Diggers, those English landless peasant communists who during the 1650s went to establish communes on abandoned land. The Diggers inspired a group of young hippie anarchists during the 1960s to start regular feedings to give food to runaway teenagers and then later inspired Food not Bombs which Carol joined to feed the homeless. She carried on that radical often forgotten English tradition both in her life and in her poetry.

In high school she was a voracious reader, devouring Dreiser, Steinbeck, Hemingway, James Farrell, Brecht, Clifford Odets. In junior college she acted in Theater of the Absurd plays, growing to like Beckett, Ionesco, and Edward Albee. On her own she read Vallejo, Breton, and Neruda. She especially liked Breton's idea about the imagination which is central to her poetry and her life. She survived the numbing jobs she worked her whole life partially by using her imagination.

Carol was a diabetic since she was a teenager. After a short-lived marriage in Marin, she moved to San Francisco, worked full-time as a secretary at UC San Francisco Medical Center while attending school at San Francisco State for six years to complete both her B.A. and M.A. "It was hard," she said. "I never want to do it again. I was exhausted." She devoted her weekends and summers to her two daughters who lived with their father in Marin.

For a short time she was on welfare, producing the enraged poem "Welfare Rights" about how men, on finding out she was on welfare, would offer her money for sex. When she graduated with her M.A., she said, "There were no full-time teaching jobs in public school system or junior college system in San Francisco. They laid off tons of people in the late '70s."

With diabetes, two children to help support, and no family back-up she couldn't get hired as an adjunct professor without benefits or job security, so she kept working as a secretary in the medical school at UC San Francisco, ran the poetry reading series at the Coffee Gallery (now the Lost and Found) in North Beach, co-founded the fiction magazine *Real Fiction*. She assisted her husband David Joseph in editing his pioneering magazine *Working Classics* featuring working class literature in the late 1980s. She was active in her union AFSCME, holding office in her local and as a delegate SF Labor Council.

At the same time as Carol was a union official in the 1980s she produced some spectacular poems about work such as "Today" celebrating having a day off with pay so she "sat in a bistro and sipped absinthe/while Cesar Vallejo strolled past,/. . . praised the sun in its holiness, led a revolution." She wrote another wonderful poem called "The Receptionist Sits at Her Desk and Hums 'Solidarity Forever.'"

Carol was a working class intellectual in the tradition of Blake and Whitman. In Carol's essay "The Making of a Working-Class Intellectual," published in *Art on the Line: Essays by Artists About the Point Where Their Art and Activism Intersect* (Curbstone, 2001), she criticized middle class people when they stereotype workers—for example, truck drivers—as "examples of ignorance and prejudice;" her father was a truck driver. She thought middle class intellectuals often lack knowledge, subtlety and nuance in their stereotypes of workers while working class people often were original thinkers.

She thought both her class and her formal education are sources of knowledge, not dividing political from artistic work. She wrote cogent literary criticism of the 1980s and 1990s poetry written largely by university professors from working class families whose poems either are nostalgic or "are often tinged with guilt and relief at having escaped the fate of their fathers by entering academia." Her own poetry lacks nostalgia or guilt but instead has a feisty sense of fighting back.

Carol criticized these bourgeois intellectuals for sentimentalizing the working class as noble sufferers. She saw no need to sentimentalize that suffering. And she added, "My heroines are those who stay [in the working class] and try to change the working conditions on their jobs." Because she wasn't upwardly mobile, she had nothing to lose by challenging middle class stereotypes and so she fought back. Carol's essay is one of the best pieces written in the last three decades on being a working class intellectual.

After the ferocious factory layoffs in the 1980s she wrote "Nellie Perkiss Speaks Her Mind" in the totally believable voice of an elderly feisty Appalachian coal miner's wife. She wrote "Work Slows Down at the Plant" about a trapped husband, fearful of losing his job, hitting his wife; the poem shows compassion for both husband and wife. Her poems broke your heart again and again.

Her first trip out of the country was to Nicaragua to witness firsthand the Sandinista Revolution. After the 1989 earthquake she spent several months traveling to Watsonville near Santa Cruz, California, where she helped feed agricultural workers and their families who had lost jobs and homes due to the earthquake's destruction.

In "As an Angel Glimpsed by Blake" she sees Blake's angel in the face of a hungry man "in a worn, black suit" who is "standing near the doorway of steel-/encased office building." She was a visionary poet like Blake, whose visions often reappear in her poems. Carol was a mystic and an activist, and she joined Food Not Bombs to feed the hungry in Civic Center, work for which she was repeatedly arrested. She introduced me to radical English culture of singer/song writers Billy Bragg and Leon Rousellon, playing for me Rousellon's two great songs "The Digger Song" (aka "The World Turned Upside Down") and "Bringing the News from Nowhere" which was about William Morris. To paraphrase Rousellon, she, like William Morris, came with a vision and walked through the river of fire.

Carol, like Whitman, was a poet for democracy. During the Gilded Age of the 1980s, 1990s and the 2000s, working people were increasing pushed aside, and she represented those who fought back with verve and passion. During this period Carol was writing a poetry necessary for America just as Whitman's poetry had been necessary for the Gilded Age of the late 19th century. To write such poetry, she adapted the poetics of the international avant-garde of Breton, Vallejo, and Neruda just as Whitman had adapted an international avant-garde poetics in an earlier generation. She knew the people she was writing about: her people she knew them in her bones. Her family. She was the warm humane beating heart of the city of San Francisco.

She had heart bypass surgery about the same time as Ferlinghetti did—knew him from North Beach where they lived the last years of her life—and compared notes with him about their surgeries. She wrote a poem about her heart disease "Recovery for the Red-Hearted Masses" answering Ginsberg's "Howl" saying "I've seen the best chests of my generation cracked and broken—Mario, Allen...." This poem is also a marvelous evocation of the North Beach she so loved. But her North Beach was made up of the working people like the poor Chinese woman with fragile bones walking against the hard wind.

Her attempts at having her work published in a full-length book of poetry were repeatedly rejected, but she did have her work circulated widely in magazines and anthologies. She was marginalized in the Bay Area literary community for writing about the working class. As the years went by and her diabetes and heart disease worsened, she lost her blonde beauty; in her fifties she walked stoop shouldered, making her even more marginalized. She knew it. Well, Whitman was marginalized. Dickinson was marginalized. They knew it, too

With worsening diabetes and heart disease, she retired from her job in January 2005, and applied for disability, as her retirement wasn't enough to live on. The insurance company turned her down, knowing full well that 80% of applications for federal disability are rejected. With her limited pension she couldn't afford to move and had to live in a third-floor walk-up in North Beach. Still, she remained active, going out daily to meet friends and family, read at poetry events and took part in demonstrations for the homeless and against the war in Iraq. She had to daily walk up the stairs to her third-floor walk-up, running out of breath on each landing as her heart disease was getting worse. June 15, 2004, she died of a heart attack.

Julia Stein, June 13, 2011

WHITE TRASH: AN AUTOBIOGRAPHY

Part I: 1948: Dysentery in the First World

My daddy was a truck driver. In Salinas he hauled lettuce.
When I was five, we lived in a three-room trailer:
my mother who played little squirrels with us
when it rained—my brother, sister and I who pretended
we lived in trees, gathered nuts and it was never winter,
we always ate—and my father who never went to high school,
who wasn't a vet because he had been kicked out
of the army on a Section 8, who once was a fireman
on the railroad, who was a Teamster,
who never crossed a picket line, never scabbed.
Our friends were Mexicans, Indians, Okies,
farmworkers, gas station attendants, taxi drivers,
carpenters, communists, ex-cons, out of work,
Red, Brown and White Trash.

We didn't have lawns, instead we shared the gravel,
the wash tubs, the showers, the toilets.
My little brother and I played in the fields
behind the trailer court.
We found an irrigation ditch to wade in.
I pushed my brother, he fell down,
stuck his hands into the slimy water,
lifted his fingers to his mouth, licked.

That night he awoke with a belly ache and diarrhea.
It lasted a week. I watched from my bunk bed
as he sat on a pot in the middle of the room,
his shit turning to blood,
blood turning to a thin clear liquid.
His ribs protruded form his white skin.
His red hair shone luminous in the dark.
Sores grew on his lips. He was all the time thirsty.

I

He went to the hospital.
After two weeks the doctors told my mother
to take him home to die.
Instead she took him to a university medical center.
He was given antibiotics and lived.

He got lots of toys.
One was a stringed horse that wobbled and danced
when you pushed the wooden knob it stood on.
His favorite was a book called *The Little Pond*.
It had pictures of animals with their faces
dipped in bright blue water:
deer, raccoon, sparrows, rabbits.
Mommy tried to read it to us when he was well,
but she always cried. She said that when he was sick
she sat by his bed day and night and
listened to him beg for water.

Summer came. The lettuce shriveled in the fields.
Daddy got laid off and we moved to Redding.
The trailer park we lived in had grass and oak trees.
In the evening, when the air cooled,
we sat with the neighbors under the oaks.
The women talked. The men played dominoes.
The children ran, pushed, shouted.
Lizards climbed our legs. Giggling, we shook them off.
Daddy lost his job. We moved to Folsom.
Hospital bills followed us up and down California.
We never paid.

Part II: Irvington Square (1958-1959)

When I was fifteen, my best friend was named Diane.
She was French Canadian and Indian,
but everyone thought she was Mexican.
Daddy drove a big diesel rig.
We lived in a house in Irvington Square. It was small,
square and painted turquoise. It had one bathroom,
a cement block tile floor and no foundation.
Our neighbors worked in the GM plant.
They were Okies and Chicanos.
All the houses were identical.
The streets were named for movie stars:
Elizabeth, Gina, Rita, Marilyn, Hudson, Hunter,
Wayne, Dean, Lancaster. I lived on Gina.
Diane's father drove up and down Irvington Square
in a blue pickup like it was a hot rod.
The girls thought he was cute. He had a duck tail.
Diane's mother was dark, thin, beautiful,
with a straight nose, small hands.
One night her father didn't come home,
but the neighbors saw him driving around with a girl
snuggled close. They said she was 16 and pregnant,
like his oldest daughter,
the one who was married to Ernie Jimenez,
the one who lived in Decoto, the one who was pregnant.
Ernie was in the joint for Mary Jane possession.

Diane and I went to the baby shower.
While her sister opened presents,
we walked around Decoto's dirt streets,
watched the children and dogs run in the road,
pretended to ignore the cute guys when they whistled.
Diane said she liked it when they called to her,
Heeey Chicana. The rest she didn't understand
because she didn't speak Spanish.
I wrote Ernie to cheer him up.

He said jail wasn't so bad because there were lots of books.
His letters were full of big words:
effervescent simultaneous coherence rapport amiability.

One day Diane's father came home, said
he wanted to see his baby son. His teenaged girlfriend
sat outside in the passenger seat of the pickup.
Diane's beautiful mother threw a milk bottle at his head.
She chased him outside with a butcher knife,
tried to open the pickup door,
slashed at the windows with the big, steel blade.
The girl locked the doors and cried.
Diane's father grabbed the knife,
threw his wife down on the asphalt,
then drove his 16 year-old pregnant lover someplace safe,
while Diane's mother chased them, screaming,
How many babies will you give her, you bastard, how many?
Diane ran after her, shouting,
Get out of the street, Mama, Mama, get inside.
The neighbors stood on their lawns. No one said anything.
Diane's little brother and sister huddled in the doorway,
crying. Diane got suspended for smoking in the bathroom.
She flunked English, General Math, Health Education.
She quit going to school. She was fifteen.
The bank foreclosed on the house. The social workers came.
Diane, her mother, little sister and brother
moved to the projects in Oakland.
Ernie got out of jail. The older sister stayed in Decoto.
Louie, the older brother,
parked his car by the Safeway and lived in it,
painted a picture of a Mohawk Indian on the passenger door.
He was 6 feet tall, with shimmering brown skin and black hair
that flowed into a waterfall over his forehead
and almost touched the arch of his long, curving nose.
Everyone called him Chief.

Part III: Two Virgins (1958)

Diane had strong, long legs that swung from wide hips.
Her brown hair was cut short and curly on top of her head
and straight in back. It fell to a point
between her shoulder blades.
She helped me cut my blonde hair the same.
Her eyes were slanted brown above her high cheekbones.
She was French Canadian and Indian.
She wanted to be Chicano.
When I first saw her I was afraid. I thought she was
Queen of the Pachucas. I thought she was bad and beautiful.
I thought she would choose me out.
I thought she would beat me up.

One evening I met her at the grocery store.
She was trying to buy cigarettes. I helped her steal a pack.
We ran to her house and locked the door. No one followed.
I stayed for dinner: Hot dogs and Hormel chili.
When it was dark we went for a walk and talked.
We walked to Mission San Jose, talking all the way.
Men and boys followed us in their cars,
asked if we needed a ride. We laughed at them,
called them ignorant fools, kept walking,
flaunted our unattainability. We were proud virgins.
The houses in Mission San Jose had family rooms, dens,
double garages, two and one-half bathrooms,
newly mowed lawns.
We pretended we were married, had three children.
We discussed what our husbands did for a living:
Fireman, auto worker, teacher (that was me),
never businessman or cop.
We chose the homes we would live in
when we were mothers, when we were married,
when our husbands brought home paychecks.

In the daytime we walked to newly constructed houses
and pretended we were buying the model with an
enclosed dining area and sunken living room.
The salesmen ignored us as we sat for hours
on the Montgomery Ward sofa.

We hiked to Niles Canyon and had a picnic.
We talked about the ghost who appeared every Halloween,
a teenaged girl killed on her way to a dance 10 years before,
who sat on a rock in the middle of Niles Creek and wept
for the children and husband she would never have,
a house with a separate dining room.

Two kids got killed driving 100 miles per hour
around the Canyon's curves. The grieving father
towed the wreck to the high school parking lot
as a lesson. Everyone stood around
looking for blood and bits of flesh, but nobody spoke.
A few hours later, when he left, he was crying.

Diane and I didn't have boyfriends with cars.
Day and night we walked. One night, as we walked on
Mission San Jose Boulevard's gravel shoulder,
a car followed us. We ignored its headlights.
It stopped. We weren't afraid. We never were afraid.
A man stepped out, said he was a cop, showed us a badge.
He asked for our names, took down our descriptions.
(Two female juveniles:
one dark, medium frame; one fair, slight frame.)
He called on his unmarked car's radio.
We checked out, we weren't runaways.
But you have a reputation for walking around, he said.
He let us go. We kept walking.

Part IV: The Projects (1960)

I took the bus to Oakland to spend the weekend with Diane.
The projects were rows of wood framed barracks,
once painted white.
Children played in the trash sprouted lawns.
Teenaged girls gathered in bunches along the sidewalks,
whispered and taunted us
as we walked past on our way to the corner store for cokes.
Diane and I sat on her front step and filed our nails.
We stared back with cold and menacing eyes
as we slowly ran the metal points over our thumbs.
Sharp dudes with slicked back black hair, thin moustaches,
their eyes covered with shades,
drove past in raked '56 Chevies.
Sunlight gleamed on the white walled tires,
silver spikes twirled from the hubcaps.
Hey Sheena, one yelled to me, you Queen of the Jungle?
I hate that blonde *puta*,
a girl hissed from across the street.
Diane and I looked at one another and filed our nails.
We didn't giggle in the presence of the enemy.
Her sister used to go steady with Johnny Moreno,
Diane whispered, but now he goes with me.

Diane walked me to the bus stop so I wouldn't get hassled.
She was wearing pedal pushers, a black sweater,
black flat-heeled shoes, no lipstick.
Her hair was in rollers.
I have a date with Johnny tonight, she explained.
She said she liked Oakland, liked the guys,
felt she belonged.
I promised to visit again, but I didn't know when.
You know, I said, school.
I thought the projects were scary, but I didn't say so.
See you around, she said, turned and walked away.
I waited for the bus by myself.
I became friends with Becky Martinez
who lived on Rita Street, but we didn't walk around.

We played records in her bedroom with the door closed.
We called boys on the phone and hung up when they answered.
The football team yelled "Yahoo, baby" at me
in the school hallways. I didn't know what they meant.
I hid in the bathroom. I was put in college preparatory classes.
The girls asked what housing tract I lived in.
When I said Irvington Square, they stopped talking to me.
When they got bad grades, they said,
Watch it, you'll end up waiting tables, or
You don't want to marry a truck driver, do you?
No one asked me to school dances.
But why? Becky asked. You're pretty. Sometimes
a boy from another school would take me to a movie.
Becky started going steady with Bobby Gomez.
I stayed home and read:
The Amboy Dukes. Knock On Any Door.
I discovered Theodore Dreiser, Richard Wright, George Orwell.
I read about drama during the Thirties.
I read *Waiting for Lefty*.
I wanted to join the Group Theater in New York.
I wanted to join Hemingway in Spain.
I wanted to read Brecht,
but he wasn't in the school library.

Louie visited. He asked to stay for supper.
He hadn't bathed in weeks.
He said Diane was pregnant.
Her boyfriend stole a car and was in jail.
Write her, he said.
I didn't. I didn't know what to say.
Becky married Bobby Gomez.
I went to junior college.

IN CIRCLED SILENCE

In circled silence
      My people came
Quiet colors, Quaker hats
In peaceful witness
They plowed their light and
Built a freedom train that
Stretched in secret from
Basement to hayloft to
A slaveless border
Gently lawless
      My people came
In circled wagons
      My people came
Quilting a pattern across
Yellowed plains and greensprung valleys
Gentle gypsies who peddled
Pots and plows and peace
These Children of the Light
Friendly Seekers
      My people came
In circled chains
      My people came
Suffragettes and pacifists
Scorned, beaten, forcefed in prison darkness
Drenching a blinded nation with their
Inward Light
Gentle Warriors
      My people came

In silenced circles
      My people came
Centuries ago
From a Europe I do not claim
These Children of the Light

They came
In peaceful witness to a
Dark skinned earth
And I am rooted to their light
I am their witness to this
America I cannot deny
I am the sound of their
Circled silence

REAL FATHER

Mama always said, "Your father
has no sense of humor."
Daddy's face ripened plumb red,
his belly shaking in waves,
splashing us with laughter
as we rushed raw and gleaming
through the lawn sprinkler.
Real Father grimaced square
jawed, narrow eyed from the
bottom of Mama's bureau. At
school we wore his name shame-
faced, me tugging the hem of my
too short dress, Robby poking
his thumb in the holes of his
red plaid flannel shirt, ex-
plaining the how comes of half
sisters, stepfathers. Robby
gave up first, registered
Daddy's name in second grade,

but I remembered an unsmiling
soldier dumping me naked
into a tub, stealing me
across state borders, leaving
me with Grandma who prayed
for my soul and burned buttocks
when I sat on a gas heater.
Uncle Les brought a big desert
turtle, didn't budge its head
from the dusty shell the whole
six weeks I waited for Mama's
and Daddy's rescue. Real Father
never returned, wrote one
postcard, two letters, sent a
photograph from Korea. Robby
cut off the head making

a paper doll, a faceless warrior
standing by a jeep, private
first class. Mailed a blue
taffeta dress one Christmas,
purple buttons running tears
down my chest the first time
Mama washed it. I didn't
wait for more presents.
Took Daddy's name in junior high
and forgot.

II
I am sitting by the window,
squinting, through glass
as afternoon sun reflects
the green glare of acacia
leaves. And I lifted
each word from his letter,
rummaging for humorous cracks
between the "I've always thought
of yous" and "It wasn't possibles."

Yes, I answered, come, not adding
Stranger, blood runs deeper than
birth certificates, is wet,
ripples in foamy, funny currents.

He will greet me flat eyed,
tight mouthed, hands hanging
limp, voice dry, untuned. I
will pour coffee from a ceramic
mug, offer homebaked molasses
cookies as I listen to arid
descriptions of L.A. freeways,
a Sears Roebuck house, arguments
in favor of military spending,
nuclear power, a war ten years
lost. Okay, Real Father.

Do we say it? Absence
makes the heart grow dead.

I know a story. I can see
a skinny, brown-haired young
man wearing regulation khaki
scoop his first-born daughter
from her crib, carry her into
sunlight, plant kisses on her
soft, blonde head, whisper,
whisper this is my dream
my dream for you. Father.
Tell me.
Is the story true?

DADDY NAPPED

by the side of the road
a dry lake bed cracked
fine lines into a
one-armed naked
      rubber doll
dumped on the landscape
& a limp bicycle tire
      we wrapped
around our waists

memory a sign with
no language or purpose
see see see

my narcoleptic daddy's
      head thrust
back across the seat thru
      the window of our
'48 blue coupe with boxes we
kids sat on upholstered
         cardboard
the road zipping beneath us
the floor's holes   this
   somehow comforts me

now I type s-i-n-g
      for s-i-g-n as in:
"sing on the dotted line"

      are dead images
mistakes from our brainwaves
      dyslexia on a floppy disk
something to wonder about
when i'm bored at work

     & the lake spreads
before me in thick caked
  layers   daddy's mouth
        slack & hanging open
      like a ? mark

THERE IS A RIVER IN ME

There is a river in me. I am
running to the sea. A tow line
connects me to a boulder lodged
in naked cliffs rising like
shoulder blades above the sand
I run to waves that break across
my bare feet, unable to reach the
depths where water lies in green
circles of light filtered through
strands of grass floating
like hair on drowned women.

My mother was not a mermaid.
She grew legs into tree trunks
and stayed planted until
the sky cracked open and birds
smashed their wings against her
bark. But I am rapids spilling
down bare rocks. I refuse to wait
on shore for the apocalypse and
resurrection.

The tide pulls. Do not try to
stop it, Mother. I am
leaving heaven to you, taking
space to dive. If I drown,
I drown.

THE EASTER BUNNY IS ALIVE AND WELL AND LIVING IN SAUSALITO WHEN HE'S NOT IN A BAR IN THE FINANCIAL DISTRICT

Good Friday spent in a
Businessman's bar
Where no one has ever stopped enjoying
World War II
And small blondes with large breasts
A middle aged fortress of
Naugahyde and Formica fantasies.
May I join you I'm a
Computer Salesman
He says as he leers at me with
Moist Impotent Eyes
I've never been joined to a
Computer Salesman before and I'm very
Democratic
What do you want in your
Easter Basket
He asks, leaking his liquored breath over me
I answer, dry and sad and laughing
I want a jade and opal sunset
I want to taste a country morning
I want to touch the bottom of the sun
I want to believe in love
I want to always be me
I want to sleep inside a laugh
Alone.
Oh, he says, and I was going to give you a
Chocolate Bunny.

Jesus Wept.

WELFARE RIGHTS

don't never tell nobody
you're on welfare
not even your

best friend he still
might dump scorn
on your face and hands
    thinking behind his

smile you're a degenerate
lay-about sloth
        dog shit and
you don't even own no
dog not being able to
purchase pet food
        with foodstamps
no baby don't even
    whisper welfare

specially when you hitch
a ride with a pressed
        and shiny pro-
fessional man or a
laboring dude with
grease stains on his pants
and they just have to
know how you live
as if your outstretched out
raggedy thumb didn't already
        say it all

and so you grunt
I get these checks in
the mail on the 1st and
15th of each month

and then by some cosmic
consciousness or just ordin-
ary street sense they
          decide you're desperate
for anything and they
leer and rub their
scorpion legs against yours
offering $10 or $400 dependin'
on what they're wearing
and you got to be polite and
innocent and lower your eyes
          real sugary

just like your mama
taught you muttering
No Thank You Sir
when you're burning up
inside and your finger-
nails just aching for
          some blood

ARGUMENTS WITH A WOULD-BE RAPIST

Untangle me
Your elbow dents my left breast and
Your knees are a Playtex girdle round my ribs
My loins are snarled in yours and I'm
Quite uncomfortable
Thank you
This is most unfair; you are penalizing me
I am a pacifist; I cannot fight you
I am an anarchist; I cannot jail you
I am a Christian; I cannot hate you
You have me crushed inside my principles
But I am female; I can outwait you
I am Woman; I can endure you
And I am unafraid
For a few minuscule plunges
You can spurt humiliation upwards into me
You can salivate on my pride
You can grind my tenderness to pulp
But you cannot rob me of my freedom
I will not be afraid
Your hipbones can batter the softness of my belly
But you cannot really touch me
You cannot have my fear
Can't you smell the shadow of my laughter?
Can't you see the coldness of my breath?
Can't you hear the dryness of my center?
I am Libran; I will outtalk you.
So why don't you just
Zip up your pants?

TO A YOUNG DANCER

You can't bend your knees,
So you cry at night, while
I pound language from a
machine. "I'm sorry"
is an empty sound, not worth
legs gone mute. In this

Chinese year of the horse,
we don't speak of justice,
or that you've been named
snake. The doctor says
Quit the dance, but I'm your
Mother and I say, CRAWL,

Light circling your new skin,
as you slide to center stage.

PT. REYES ODE
for David

Yesterday, before dawn, we awoke
to blue jays screaming, a joyous
playful squabble that broke
through our nylon tent. Close
and warm in down bags, we
laughed, complained of rocks, then
slept again until sun melted
the wet sky and moisture seeped
over our yellow roof, spinning
webs of cold liquid that smelt

clean and salty. I grabbed
your hand as we walked
the beach, pebbles stabbing
our shoes, the sand flecked
with white, glistening foam.
Deer grazed meadow grass
sprouting from the hills above
Coast Camp, snakes flashed
underfoot and lizards combed
the tangled berry bushes hover-

ing against the narrow trail
that led us to the highway, back
to asphalt, cars, small failures
in the transit system, the cracks
in our politics, our petty aches,
our loneliness. We no longer
touched, our thumbs pleading
for a ride that would take
us home to strangers
waiting in bus stops, leaving
sun and quiet to hawks, lupine,
manzanitas, larkspur, the mute
hard ground, morning glories winding

over granite cliffs. They'll shoot
the deer at Pt. Reyes. Overbred,
unchecked, unafraid, they eat
too much. I can't feel
pity. What's one dead
deer? It was the Greeks
invented harmony and they killed
as well as any race. Tonight,
when I dream again of prisons,
barbed wire, searching lights,
I'll reach for your sunburned skin,
my fingers climbing your thighs,
digging comfort from human
soil, because I want to live
with myself. You will rise
to my hands. Celebrating one
another, we will learn to forgive.

SMALL DEATHS

I tear my hair like the mad
.........queen of hearts. "What? You.
.........used a whole cube of butter
.........to fry one egg?" Leah's eyes drop;
.........I refuse to see the lashes cast
.........shadows on her cheeks, too busy
.........thinking, I must wipe dust
.........from under the coffee table, and
.........I'm tired, my gaze sagging on the
.........electric wires splintering
.........the pale blue sky. Her voice
.........trembles, "I'll go to the store,
.........Mommy, and buy it with my allowance."
.........Another small death, this time caused
.........by the misappropriation of fifty
.........cents worth of cholesterol.

Last night my obscene "friend"
.........called to awake me with silence.
.........The telephone company will charge
.........eleven dollars for a new number.
.........Friday the boss will sign my
.........paycheck at three minutes past
.........five. The bank opens at ten a.m.
.........Monday morning. This weekend
.........marks our conversion to
.........vegetarianism, Sunday dinners
.........of brown rice, inexpensive
.........walks on the beach to quiet
.........our taste for blood. And
.........this evening, when the bus
.........winds up and down city hills,
.........pushing me closer to my 5/6ths
.........psychiatric hour, when I will
.........discuss the hostility inherent
.........in my passively aggressive

.........overdue bill, I will be grateful
.........for a seat by the window;

.........I will be grateful for the sun's
.........heat on my cheek, its light
.........slipping through the yellow
.........and red strands of hair that
.........I stretch around my fingers
.........so that I may sing
.........there are rainbows in me yet.
.........I am pulling the cord, stepping
.........onto littered sidewalks, furtively
.........searching for two-way mirrors,
.........hidden microphones as I slouch
.........on the therapeutic chair, pleading:

   GUILTY AS CHARGED!
Guilty of screaming at my child
Guilty of stealing the office stamps
Conspiring to cheat Landlords of Cleaning Deposits
Writing Rhetorical Poems with no Metaphorical Content
Refusing to tend my garden, instead
Proclaiming the aesthetic purity of weeds
Guilty even of the inability to fantasize rape
The nonownership of a vibrator
Yes I am guilty of
Refraining from reading the NYSE Daily Quotations
Choosing instead to watch fog seep through the heavy
branches of cypress trees, dark green foliage wetted
darker green. Yes! Yes!
Guilty of the desire to raise my fist to Montgomery Street's
skyscraped glare, shouting "Next Year In Madrid!"
And most of all
Guilty of keeping my mouth shut
Crossing my legs in public
Ignoring the wind's cry as it sweeps grease
from tankers mounting the ocean's dying waves.

.........The doctor wipes his glasses on his
.........imported Italian shirt and suggests
.........redefining options,
.........acceptance of limitations,
.........a course in assertiveness training.
.........I shrink back on the cushions and
.........cop a plea. "Nolo contendere."

.........I am thrusting the key in the
.........hole, turning its toothy blade.
.........Leah is linking her hands
.........around my belly. I flop
.........rag dolled on the couch as
.........she removes my shoes, her
.........fleshly padded fingers de-
.........manding "Play with me."
.........It's no game, kid, this living,
.........no accident that profit
.........is mined from dirty phone calls.
.........Okay, pumpkin, do I bury you
.........with the wasted butter,
.........or do we buy guns? You're
.........right. It's too early
.........to go to bed. Even fifth
.........graders know the earth is not
.........a pyramid, but a porous,
.........shimmering egg dropped
.........monthly from between our legs,
.........giving and taking the pounding
.........of our feet as we dance
.........round and round, sweat
.........circling our throats, our faces
.........lifted to the moon dripping
.........juicy on our tongues flagging
.........cars that screech past
.........the window, yes, our wet, red,
.........throbbing anarchist tongues

LEAH'S SONG

The sun dances down the mountain
The rain whispers through the trees
The wind races the river to the sea
The day has finished its song

DEREK DABROSKI: THE PEOPLE'S HERO

My grandson wants me
to write him a poem.
He also wants *Mad Magazine*,
hikes in the woods,
swimming lessons, art supplies,
world peace, and economic justice.
Most of all he would like
a computer game about killing.
It's only pretend, he says.
I don't like bombing real people.
His hazel eyes appraise my naivety
with disgust and suspicion.
He complains when I insist
he wear a bicycle helmet.
It's my only rule, I explain.
You forgot about war,
he shouts as he pedals
down the North Beach sidewalk,
his skinny legs pumping
faster and faster.

We sit on the grass
in Washington Square Park,
catch our breath,
watch three policemen
yank a man out of his sleep,
drag him to a paddy wagon.
I want to tell Derek
about a World War II photograph
of a boy, arms raised,
a rifle barrel pointed at his head,
staring into the camera,
horror imprinted on his small face.

I stroke Derek's cheek,
seeking explanations and comfort,
but he grins and says,
I whispered at those cops,
See you in hell.
Then he jumps on his red bike
and races me home.

Why I Am Still a Secretary

The conference over, she meets me
at a bar. "It's out there," she
says, "if you want it bad enough."
She wraps me in her warm smile;
dimples crease her cheeks
like sacred promises. What she wants
is tenure at a community college.
Tomorrow she returns to her room
in her parents' house, her temporary
job teaching English to immigrants.

I'm hard. Bitter. My worst sin—
beyond pride, arrogance, intolerance—
an inability to respect my talents.
The last time I moved,
I accidentally threw out my degree.
I give realistic appraisals
of employment prospects as the bartender
sweeps my dollar tip into his fist.
"It's a buyer's market," I say. "It is
if you don't believe," she answers.

At work the receptionist is anxious.
"Something weird's appeared in my
mammogram. It's probably nothing."
She forgets messages, misspells names,
takes too many breaks. A week later
she's in tears. "I have no one.
Who will take care of my child?"

I drive her to the hospital,
buy her flowers, make her a card.
"You're so kind," she says.

She misses a few days' work.
I spend my lunch hour delivering
pizza to her apartment. There
is one television in the living room
and two in the bedroom she shares
with her son. His school picture
is scotchtaped to the otherwise
bare walls. "I can't sleep," she says.
"But don't worry. I'll be back at my
desk. I really need this job."

THE LIBERAL BOSS

It was, finally, all she wanted
to be alone
in the back conference room
her empty desk mocking
her silent telephone
her supervisor's anxious face
desperate to delegate
a rush job xeroxing
twenty-three travel vouchers
and their supporting documentation

the privacy to shed tears
like undergarments
before embracing
a lover who politely disappears
when the alarm rings
without demanding a cup of coffee

why are you in here
the chairman asks
and why are you crying
he clasps a bulging
manilla envelope

because, above my Premium II
386SX/20 megahertz computer,
there is a hole
in the ozone layer
the size of my heart
slowly opening up to heaven
which isn't all
it's cracked up to be

and besides, my friends
are dying of disparate diseases
my fingers no longer
grasp pleasure
or caress pain
I never sleep at night anymore
the sun is my enemy
I am an unwanted planet
without a moon, in fact,
without an orbit

I see, he says, is there
anything I can do
he waits the length of time
it takes
for the rhythmic contraction
of a heartbeat
by which blood is forced
onward, then asks

if she can transcribe the tape
he has placed on her desk
so that he can sign the letter
and she can get it in the mail
before noon

As an Employee of the University, the Clerical Worker Acknowledges Truth and Beauty

every day is an act of resistance
she thinks as she looks away
from the blinking green
alphabet and out the window.
streetcar wires cut the sky.
she likes movies about subways,
calls them underground flicks.
her word processor is beeping.
if she presses the message key,
"incorrect tab stops" will flash
across the screen's bottom.
she refuses, stares at eucalyptus
leaves rippling in the wind.
when asked if she has bought
cookies for the faculty meeting,
she laughs and does not
turn away from the trees.

SHE SITS IN THE OWL AND MONKEY CAFÉ ON HER LUNCH HOUR AND READS THE *CHRONICLE*

she forgot her glasses.
the words are splintered
on the page. the woman
in a scarlet coat
at the next table talks
with her mouth full
of bagel and cream cheese.
"all transformers are the same
color and I just thought
what a waste."
jazz mumbles from the kitchen.
newsprint rubs off on her hands.
she buries her face in her paper,
imagines black smudging her nose,
frontpage headlines inked
on her forehead.
DESPERATE FARMERS TURNING VIOLENT
ELDERLY STORM CITY HALL
SAN DIEGO MAYOR GETS ONE YEAR JAIL TERM
"they look like robots."
the woman's voice is creamy.
"I was appalled."
she skips the editorials
and letters to the editor.
the woman rises.
the hem of the coat
brushes against her leg.
she dips her spoon into her bowl,
discovers her soup is cold.
in her salad the slices
of purple cabbage
look like typos.

San Francisco
December 11, 1985

35

INFLATION ACHIEVES A SINGLE DIGIT
UNEMPLOYMENT RISES TO 8.9%

Our hands complain of protein deficiency as
David slices more than his ration of ham
5-1/2 lbs of meat per person per month in Poland
Pass the navy beans, please
They are pale pink and slushy
Legumes are good for the soul
The free enterprise of well-balanced amino acids
The dialectics of eating
Alicia denounces bland cabbage soup
History gets a C- at our fashionably
Bourgeois Butcher Block Table
When the grade drops to D+
We steal a loaf of bread
Then we build barricades

THE RECEPTIONIST SITS AT HER DESK AND HUMS "SOLIDARITY FOREVER"

we will bring to birth a new world
from the ashes of the old
— Ralph Chaplin, "Solidarity Forever"

I am the large gold fish you peeked at
through the cold rain
into the algae green pond.
My flesh has seen the four corners
of the earth. I am succulent.
My scales gleam into your
watery gray eyes.
I am the carefully placed objet d'art
that makes your phone calls,
types reports of your tax deductible
winter cruise,
greets your clients with
an oleander smile.
When I sit in my newly upholstered
swivel armless chair,
I dream of exotic locales,
walk in vast landscaped parks.
In midst I see myself
bent and old, a scarf around
my narrow shoulders,
digging in smoldering ashes,
but then I see
that I am wide hipped, tall, strong,
legs spread,
birthing.

TODAY

Today I slept until the sun eased
under my eyelashes. The office phone
rang and rang. No one answered.
Today I wrote songs for dead poets,
danced to Schubert's 8th Symphony,
(which he never had time to finish),
right leg turning *andante con moto,*
arms sweeping the ceiling as leaves fell,
green and golden, autumn in Paris.
I sat in a bistro and sipped absinthe
while Cesar Vallejo strolled past,
his dignity betrayed by the hole
in his pants, and I waved, today

and the dictaphone did not dictate
and the files remained empty
and the boss's coffee cup remained empty
while the ghosts of my ancestors
occupied my chair and threatened all
who disturbed their slumber

today, when I sat in bed, nibbling
croissants and reading the New Yorker
in San Francisco, and I did not make
my daughter's lunch, I did not pay
the PG&E bill, I did not empty the garbage
on my way out the door to catch the bus to
ride the elevator to sit at my desk on time
because today I took the day off.

And rain drenched the skins of lepers
and they were healed.
Red flags decorated the doorways
of senior centers, and everyone
received their social
security checks on time.
And I walked the streets at 10
in the morning, praised the sun
in its holiness, led a revolution,
painted my toenails purple,
meditated in solitude,
today, on this day, when I took,
with pay, the day off.

Downsizing Blues, Or, On a Bad Work Day You Can Scream Forever

It's all my fault
I wrote the wrong date
on the departmental grant
xeroxed the appendix crooked
collated the pages backwards
AND YOU DIDN'T FIRE ME!

I owe you everything:
my health benefits
three week paid vacation
my cluttered desk
carpal tunnel syndrome
the throbbing pain in my hands
the surgical scar
that lengthens
the lifeline on my palm

I agree—I need
more callouses
on my knees
so grateful am I
to have survived
the office purge
keep me out of the food stamp lines
and I'll promise to bow
till my face scrapes
the rough twill
of the gray carpet
while never ceasing to smile
thank you thank you thank you

It's 'cause we're scared
we eat the air
that poisons us
In starving times
even a killer dog
will lick the hand
that beats it

HIGH-STEPPING DOWN MONTGOMERY STREET

Feet slapping concrete,
I check my watch
at each corner,
step into the street
before the light turns green.
At Clay, two old men stride past,
one small and straight,
the other stooped into a right angle.

"I was shoveling shit so fast and hard
I was buried in sweat," he says.
His knees crease his red checkered pants.
His friend in golf cap
and pale blue windbreaker replies.
"No, you wasn't buried in sweat.
You was drownin'.
You get buried in dirt."
"I was buried in that too,"
the man says, his frail bones
curving in the morning breeze.
"My skin was sweatin' dirt."

Listening, I see them
hauling cargo off a wooden pier,
bananas flung over their shoulders,
slouched on folding chairs in hiring halls,
hands flying, cigarette smoke hurling
through crowded union meetings,
drinking alone in a small room,
waiting for the next ship, next port,
bent over a shovel,
breaking the hard ground,
stooping in asparagus fields,
the sun wrapping its flaming arms
around their bent backs.

Glimmers of sunlight sneak past
skyscraped shadows.
At the corner of Sutter,
Charles Schwab announces
in flashing yellow lights
the time, temperature,
Dow Jones daily averages.

"A bull market,"
says the doubled man.
"Bullshit," says his friend.
"Wall Street never gave you nothin'."
"That's right, Charlie.
But we still got our legs,"
the old man answers
as they stand at the curb,
watch a BMW run a red light.

I hurry across the street,
push through shiny brass and glass
revolving doors,
turn on my computer,
slouch at my desk,
squint into a glaring VDT screen,
read my e-mail.

Dear Ms. Shaw

Patricia Shaw
666 Susan Drive, Apt. B
Anthonyville, FL 65656

This letter is to inform you that due to budget cuts and reduction of assigned duties, your position as Mother has been eliminated. With the advent of new technology, as well as bottom line economic policies, it has become necessary to transfer funds previously allocated for nurture and care of loved ones to other uses. While retraining is possible with some former family members, the onset of Alzheimer's Disease combined with crippling arthritis has decreased your functioning capabilities. It is an unfortunate reality, but the demands of today's market require skill, speed and flexibility.

You are now eligible for recall and preferential rehire if a position for which you are qualified becomes available. However, I must inform you that the technological revolution presently occurring in the field of familial relations has made motherhood obsolete.

Management is always deemed necessary in a capitalist market; therefore, if you have a sex change, you may apply for employment as father provided you are qualified for the position.

This letter does not release you from your obligations as parent to provide for the well being of adult family members. Any wills and/or codicils with your signature appended are legal and binding.

This notification in no way effects your seniority rights. However, the corporation has filed suit in the US Civil Court and will not honor these rights as long as litigation is pending.

Thank you for your many decades of service to the family.

Sincerely,

Carol Shaw
President
Shaw Family, Inc.

While Watching the Clock at Work, I Contemplate the End of Entropy

And what will the rapture look like?
Will files dissolve into dust devils
and swirl off my desk
leaving piles of ashes beside the phone?
Will invoices melt in the xerox?
Will I have time to fax the kidney of a bat
to an organ bank
and demand an immediate finder's fee?
Yes! And my computer will refuse to backspace;
I will scatter my typos like bones;
while my immediate supervisor and the CEO
nip at my heels like a pack of half-dead dogs.
I will eat the appointment calendar for lunch,
and, in a bulimic fury,
toss it down the office toilet,
dreams of corporate mergers
swimming with the sewer rats.
Oh orgasmic ecstasy!
Oh joyous rain falling on my aching skin!
I am placing a personal phone call to Gabriel,
deleting the memories of a thousand machines,
ripping the chains from my ankles,
kicking off my correctly office attired one-inch heels,
my bare feet dangling delicately
above my personal bulletin board
(decorated with pictures of Brecht, Marley and Isadora)
as I gloriously rise to paradise
and join the Angels Liberation Front!

THANK YOU FOR YOUR 15 YEARS OF SERVICE TO THE DEPARTMENT

pink slipped into oblivion
the supervisor kindly grants me
permission to use
the office laser printer
to update my resume

under skills
I list my liabilities
       *age
       *attitude
       *little software knowledge
       *lack of hard drive

with clarity as searing
as sunglare on water
I write this poem
this last day
on company time

As an Angel Glimpsed by Blake

Standing near the doorway of a steel-
encased office building, the man
in the worn, black suit
wipes soil from his frayed, white
starched cuffs and waits
for his son to enter, eyes lowered,
as the man, too, lowers his eyes.
This is the best he has,
the poverty he wears, his empty hands
a gift of shame for a son
who looks away.

I see the old man
in a darkened theater,
an image superimposed on scenes
of a filmed revolution,
slipping between shadows that fall
on slogan-plastered walls.
He is my vision, my DNA chain;
I circle my wrists with his hunger
that shimmers beneath my skin
translucent like a beached jellyfish
on oil-slicked sand.

SISTERS IN THE FLAMES
for my daughter Leah

"...spectators saw again and again pitiable companionships formed in the instant of death—girls who placed their arms around each other as they leaped. In many cases their clothing was flaming or their hair flaring as they fell."

from "The Triangle Fire," The New York World, March 26, 1911

Greenhorn
bent over the machine
your hair a mess of red curls
like flames I said
my words extinguished
by the wailing motors
we never spoke
together we sewed
fine linen shirtwaists
for fine ladies we worked
in our coarse gowns and
muslin aprons 12 hours
in dark dank rooms
nine floors above the street
our fingers worked
the soft cloth
our coarse hands
fed the machines

Stranger
I saw you once in the elevator
going down going home
your eyes laughed
when I whispered too loud
strands of red hair falling
over your cheek and neck I
touched your red rough hand
my shoulders ached
my pay envelope tucked
in my coat pocket

for Papa for Mama
for the rent I need
a new skirt I need
a day in the sun
I need to unlock the doors
of this factory
I'm still young
I whispered and you laughed
because of course
we all were young

Sister
of the flames
take my hand
I will hold you in the cradle
of my billowing skirt
in the ache of my shoulders
the center of my palm
our sisters already dance
on the sidewalk nine
floors below the fire
is leaping through my hair
the air will lick our thighs
Sister together now fly
the sky is an unlocked door
and the machines are burning

THE BUTTERFLY PIN

like a teenager too shy to show
happiness or desire
she waits in line in the cold
for hot soup served in a styrofoam cup
She wears a yellow polyester jacket
and a scarf tied under her chin
when I place a slice of bread
in her small hands
she gives me
a pink enamel butterfly pin
with sequin eyes
a donation she whispers
I don't know her name
or her children's names
or if she has children
I don't remember her existence
most of the time
but I hide the gaudy treasure
so that, on those days
when smog eats the lining of the sky
I can reach into the pocket
of my levi jacket
and finger its broken clasp

NELLIE PERKISS SPEAKS HER MIND

Look at that T.V. set stretch
their faces into rubber masks.
They're my friends and family.
I'd be standing by that hole
myself, but I got too old
to wait and mourn. These
bones sounds like dry leaves
blowing in a hot wind every
time I raise myself jest to
poke the coals burning in the
stove. The news don't never
tell the way it really is.

I know some stories and I
can sing some songs. Joey
says I talk too much. Didn't
used to, not when they dumped
my Ben on the bed, his face
fulla gunshot, blood pouring
out of his mouth, cause he
was picketing the wrong boss,
that's what they said, but
next day I walked that line.

Then it was jest me and Pa,
him coughing spit black as
lava out of his sunken chest.
Weighed 110 lbs. when we buried
him, and he had been a big man,
lifting me above his head,
laughing as my white veil
stuck on his red, stubby
beard, saying I gotta be a
real woman to marry a man
tunnels the earth deep, me
jest sixteen but strong.

Now I'm so weak Joey's gotta
carry the grocery bag up the
steps and onto the kitchen
table, but he don't mind when
I give him some homebaked
rhubarb pie. Calls me Ma Perkiss
though he knows I ain't never had
no kids, not marrying again and
the girl born still six months
after Ben's funeral.

Always somebody needing me,
a new widow or busted up
organizer. Someone always
calling me Ma. When my eyes
first spotted Joey, I knowed
he'd go digging like all the
men I ever seen with hair
the color of burning coal
and freckles so bright even
mine dust couldn't wipe them
out. Was reading bout last
week's disaster up in Bellingham
when the whistle blew. The
company stoolie telling how
safety violations didn't cause
no cave-in and then that

familiar scream and me hearing
my own voice over and over saying
I won't wait for them to bring
up Joey. I won't stand in silence
while the earth spews poison gases,
only dirt don't know it's killing
the wrong ones. I'll sit here
watching T.V. interviews with
gray-suited presidents denying
they stuff death in their

wallets, and I'll take my pen,
write newspapers and politicians,
only no one's going to listen to
an old woman's lived too long,
but I tell you this, like I told
Joey, I ain't so old I can't
remember.

Work Slows Down at the Plant

Not even winter's dawning light
leaks through the screen's ripped
seams. The garden is bolted shut
by a solid storm door, the ground
cracked with ice and dead weeds.
She yawns under the kitchen's

dim bulb, slaps bread slices in
the toaster, then spreads her
palm across a curving belly. It
flutters like a butterfly, she
thinks, and smiles, but he folds
his eyes into the black humidity

of his first cup of coffee. If
he looks up, he'll see the purple
swell sprouting on her left cheek
and remember how afraid he was
when she asked if they could
plant nasturtiums next spring.

He calculated the cost of seed
packets, seeing their brilliant
golds and oranges spell last
year 35 cents, next year 50, to-
morrow laid off, next week car
insurance due and the walk needs

shoveling before work at 6 a.m.
If he could speak, he'd say last
summer his fingers opened the petals
of a rose, touched the stamen, but
this winter his fist closed. He
pulls his lunch pail from the re-

frigerator and walks out the garage
door to find the shovel, hear its
blade scrape snow like the slow
shuffle of his wife's feet as she
clears the table, sweeps the floor,
waits for the car to start, the

day to end, the child to come. Do
not wait, he whispers. Listen to
my breath. It lies frozen in my
mouth. Sleep warm and curled into
your rounding flesh, but sleep alone
tonight. Before he enters the cold

to clean the driveway, go to work,
avoid the neighbors' accusing stares—
Hey Tony your wife how come she's
hurting again—he presses his hand
against his crotch, rubs the lifeless
root, chatters tomorrow—do not wait.

PARA LOS MUCHACHOS DE NICARAGUA

I give you corn;
I give you comets that fall from a battered sky.
I cannot give you memories or gravestones.
I am the dress that is always worn for your desire;
I am the woman of the sun.

Reality aggravates
this cold ground where all the adolescents
congregate to hear Sandino
dance rhetoric into ornate circles,
tormenting those who prey on youth,
describing human atmospheres,
a land of free soil, free butterflies!

And death? Open all the windows!
And life? Open the portals of death!
Let it flow to the earth's bowels.
Hierarchy is a disgrace to free peoples!
Today we negotiate with life!

MISSION POET BANNED BY STATE DEPARTMENT

In 1976, when Roberto Vargas was serving as the director of San
Francisco's U.S. Bicentennial Celebration, he was quietly preparing
to fight in Nicaragua. He trained for the mountainous terrain by
running up Bernal Heights.

North Mission News, July 1986

Hordes of San Francisco Revolutionary poets
are invading Bernal Heights
in Birkenstocks and sneakers
made in the People's Republic of China,
their iambs and similes
like a red sea of banners.

All Metaphors to the People!
Revolution in the name of Poetry!

Up they go,
rounding the corner to Costa Street,
also known as Dog Patch
where once upon a time
a woman in a blue bathrobe
stood in front of a bulldozer
when property rights disturbed
her Saturday a.m. and secretaries,
waitresses, filmmakers, union
organizers, welfare recipients,
kids of all sizes, creeds and colors,
the unemployed, and God only knows
Marxist poets even
circled the contractor, the land
owner and the real estate agent,
hurling epitaphs and insults:

Down With Upward Mobility!
Mister, Leave Our Shacks Alone!

Past the bulldozer and blue
bathrobe, past lazy dogs
sleeping on unpaved streets,
up the hill, there they go
—Revolutionary Poets—
flashing their small press books,
their heavy breath blazing
the sky with image clusters,

Mayakovski's and Neruda's
tender bastards,
illegitimacy being the legitimate
response to property and state.

Give me a Trope! Give me a Rhyme!
Join the Revolution! Make this Climb!

For our comrade, Roberto Vargas, Exiled San Francisco
Poet and Citizen of Nicaragua Libre

RECOVERY FOR THE RED-HEARTED MASSES

Skateboards gyrate under my window.
A child is squealing.
A street fair's booths are bursting
With America's bright foliage
Of consumer goods I can't afford.
It's the Recovery!
Corn on the Cob in America!
Even the pigeons are gloating!
Last week Geronimo Pratt was freed
And we stood outside his prison gates
Screaming Open Sesame! Magic happens
If you work at it for 26 years.
Free Mumia! It could happen yet.

Monday I walk to work past Crazy Mary
Who lives in the doorways
Of San Francisco's empty storefronts.
On payday I give her some quarters,
A piece of fruit, a candy bar.
A redbrowned smile burns in her face.
Dirt splatters ripped hands that hold
A battered quart of half-empty milk.
"I'm not crazy," she says, then laughs.
"You wear junk jewelry.
I know real stones when I see them."

New stores are shooting up like
Wildflowers in a spring rain.
Crazy Mary moves on,
The streets swept clean by her absence.
"It's not progress," she cries,
Her back receding down the street.
"It's lonely."
Wind whips her skirts

Around her thin legs.
The clouded sky turns gray.
Water puddles around my shoes.

The Transamerica building
Is turning cartwheels above my head.
My breath is jerking out of my lungs.
My chest bumps and grinds its way across Broadway.
I grab a cab to Kaiser ER.
Oh my god—I've seen
The best chests of my generation
Cracked and broken—Mario, Allen—
I sign the papers. I volunteer.
It's by-pass time!

Fire in Waco! Explosions in Oklahoma!
Lethal injections in Texas!
The gurney slips me oh so steadily
towards the surgeon's saw.
And all I can think of is
I feel sorry for the worst minds
Of America. Pity the fool
Who in her last moments
Pities her executioner.

Three months later I'm still
Walking these hard streets.
Crazy Mary's gone.
Young exiles from suburbia
Wearing shorts and baseball caps
Block my way up the hill
To my one-room apartment.
Microbrew slurps onto their T-shirts
Advertising Nike slave wear.
Bill Gates leaks out of their half-dead eyes.
Escaped inmates from Phi Beta Puka.

"Get outa North Beach," I shout,
"Leave us poor and loony folk alone!"
But they don't see me.

They don't see the Chinese grandmother
Crossing the street with a baby strapped
To her back, her frail bones
Bending in the wind.

They don't see the three black men
Clapping desperately for coins,
Their voices do-wopping,
"While I was praying,
somebody touched me."
They don't see the Latino immigrants
Evicted from their North Beach Public Housing.
They don't see the Lusty Ladies holding
A union meeting at the Dark Horse Coffee House.
What do they see? Real Estate?
Another sports bar?
Oh Crazy Mary, where have they buried you?

I finally make it past City Lights.
My heart is a pressure cooker.
My twisted breath cracks against my ribs.
My friend Jack steps out of Specs,
Crosses the street, takes me inside Vesuvios,
Gets me water.
"I've sold six *People's Tribunes*," he grins.
His gray hair, streaked with yellow,
Gathers around his red sweater's neckline.
"I'm tired of everything," I say.
He smiles and reads me his latest poem
About the city's janitors
And their giant moustache brooms
Sweeping San Francisco bright and beautiful.
I rise with the brooms.
I rise with the janitors.

My heart is quiet.
My heart will carry me
The rest of the way home,
My crazy, dancing heart,
My sweeping heart,
My aching heart,
My breaking heart
My still beating
Red red heart.

BELIEVE IN MY HANDS (WHICH ARE ENDING)

for Silvio Rodriguez of Cuba

At the end of my hands
is the face of a child
whose right eye is planted
in the center of her pale cheekbone.

At the edge of my fingers,
pacing beneath a movie marquee,
is an old man in a red cap on whose
shoulder blossoms a picket sign.

The rain he stands in defines
the limits of my hands. Still
I trust in the slick, wet pavement
where my body ends,

but where my imagination
explodes into white carnations.
I believe in the thick, black dirt
that sifts through my closed fist.

I believe in the child whose
deformed face is a luminous moon.
I believe in the hot sun where
a revolution was named for a poet.

I trust in the mystery of future
which is always beginning.

Jack Hirschman is a San Francisco poet, translator, and editor. His powerfully eloquent voice set the tone for political poetry in this country many years ago. Since leaving a teaching career in the '60s, Hirschman has taken the free exchange of poetry and politics into the streets where he is, in the words of poet Luke Breit, "America's most important living poet." He is the author of numerous books of poetry, plus some 45 translations from a half a dozen languages, as well as the editor of anthologies and journals. Among his many volumes of poetry are *Endless Threshold, The Xibalba Arcane, Lyripol* (City Lights, 1976) and *All That's Left* (City Lights, 2008). (Bio courtesy City Lights Booksellers & Publishers)

Julia Stein has published four books of poetry: *Under the Ladder to Heaven* (West End Press, 1984), *Desert Soldiers* (California Classics, 1992), *Shulamith* (West End Press, 2002), and *Walker Woman* (West End Press, 2001). She edited the anthology *Walking Through a River of Fire: 100 Years of Triangle Fire Poetry* (CC Marimbo, 2011). She is also a union activist and tireless advocate for working class issues and concerns.

David Joseph shared with Carol Tarlen, during their marriage of 14 years, the writing life and activism and advocacy for working class people. He edited *Working Classics*, a magazine which published literary work by and for working people. His poetry and prose have appeared in numerous journals including *Rolling Stone, SF Review of Books, The News from Nowhere, Aguas Calientes, Mockingbird, Samisdat, Beatitude* and *Iron*. In 2007 he was selected for the Friends of the San Francisco Public Library Poets 11 Poetry Prize.

Carol Tarlen's poetry and prose were published in literary journals (*Ikon, Exquisite Corpse, The Berkley Poetry Review, Sing Heavenly Muse, Hurricane Alice, Poetry USA*) and in four anthologies: *Calling Home: Writings of Working Class Women* (Rutgers University Press); *Liberating Memory* (Rutgers University Press); *American Working-Class Literature* (Oxford UP) and *For A Living* (University of Illinois Press). In 1994, she was the first place winner in the San Francisco Bay Guardian Poetry Contest. She was active for many years in labor, peace, and homeless advocacy groups. Ms Tarlen died in 2004.

www.ingramcontent.com/pod-product-compliance
Lightning Source LLC
La Vergne TN
LVHW051605080426
835510LV00020B/3147